Each time you see a flag in a picture, it is a Paper Puzzler. Try to find what is made of paper in the picture. The answers are on pages 30, 31, and 32.

VOYAGER BOOKS
HARCOURT BRACE & COMPANY
San Diego   New York   London

Gail Gibbons

PAPER, PAPER EVERYWHERE

FOR BURT BESEN

PAPER PUZZLER

First Voyager Books edition 1997
Voyager Books is a registered trademark of Harcourt Brace & Company.

Library of Congress Cataloging-in-Publication Data
Gibbons, Gail.   Paper, paper everywhere.
Summary: Briefly discusses where paper comes from, how it is made, and how we use it.
1. Paper — Juvenile literature.   [1. Paper]   I. Title.
TS1105.5.G5   676'.2   82-3109
ISBN 0-15-259488-4   ISBN 0-15-201491-8 (pbk.)

Grateful acknowledgment for their professional advice is made to
Tom Purple, Andy Beckwith, and John Watson—paper people all.

A C E F D B

Printed in Singapore

Paper is everywhere.

At a picnic we use paper.

We play trick or treat with paper at Halloween.

At a birthday party we find paper . . .

and at school, too. But where does paper come from?

Most paper comes from trees.

People called lumberjacks go into the forests.

There they cut down different kinds of trees and saw off the branches.

The logs are loaded onto trucks, which take them to a paper mill.

15

Bark is scraped off the logs in a large round drum.
The clean logs are thrown onto a conveyor belt.

The belt takes the logs to another machine,
where they are cut into tiny chips.

The next stop is a vat, where the chips, cooked in chemicals, fall apart into tiny fibers called pulp.

The pulp is washed . . .

and bleached . . .

and stirred until it is a smooth, watery mixture.

This mixture is poured onto a flat moving screen, which is part of a paper-making machine as long as a football field.

As the mixture moves along the vibrating screen, some of the water drains away, and the pulp becomes very wet paper.

As the paper is squeezed between huge rollers,
more water is pressed out.

24

In the next step, the long, smooth web of paper is dried as it moves over and under hot rollers.

Then the paper is wound into big rolls.

Some of the rolls are cut into sheets.

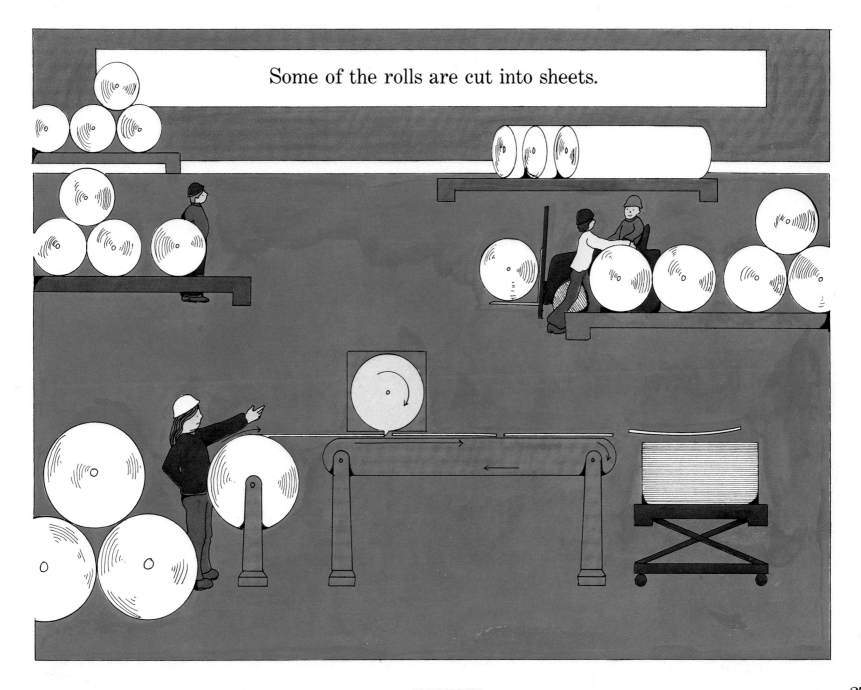

After the paper is inspected . . .

it is shipped to printing plants and factories everywhere to make books, streamers, newspapers, napkins, kites, paper hats, notebooks, masks, and other paper products we use every day.

Page 1

Pages 2–3

The paper in this book was made using the method described in this book. Some other types of paper are made from rags, cotton, or recycled wastepaper. They are made by a similar process.

This book was designed by Barbara DuPree Knowles. It was set in Century Expanded and printed and bound by Horowitz/Rae Book Manufacturers, Fairfield, New Jersey.

The preseparated art was prepared in shades of gray paint laid over ink line.

This book was printed on Leykam recycled paper, which contains more than 20 percent postconsumer waste and has a total recycled content of at least 50 percent.